TELL ME ABOUT PIONEERS

FLORENCE NIGHTINGALE

written by
John Malam

Evans

500 800983

Contact the Author

Tell me what you think about this book.
Write to me at Evans Brothers.
Or e-mail me at: johnmalam@aol.com

Internet information

www.florence-nightingale.co.uk
The Florence Nightingale Museum,
London.

www.ushsdolls.com/paperdoll/pdfa.htm
A Florence Nightingale paper doll to
print out and make.

www.countryjoe.com/nightingale
/index.html
Florence Nightingale's life in words and
pictures, plus a sound recording of her
voice recorded in London in the year
1890. She can be heard saying:

"When I am no longer even a memory,
just a name, I hope my voice may
perpetuate the great work of my life.
God bless my dear old comrades of
Balaclava and bring them safe to
shore."

VISIT OUR WEBSITE
www.evansbooks.co.uk
Evans

Published by Evans Brothers Limited
2A Portman Mansions
Chiltern Street
London W1U 6NR

© Evans Brothers Limited 2003

First published 2003

Printed in Hong Kong by Wing King Tong Co. Ltd.

British Library Cataloguing in Publication data.

Malam, John
   Tell me about Florence Nightingale
   1. Nightingale, Florence 1820-1910 - Juvenile literature
   2. Nurses - England - Biography - Juvenile literature
   3. Crimean War, 1853-1856 - Medical care - Great Britain -
   Juvenile literature
   I. Title II. Florence Nightingale
   610.7'3'092

ISBN 0237524767

Florence Nightingale was the founder of modern nursing. She devoted her life to changing the way the sick were cared for and made people realise that nurses did important work. This is her story.

Florence Nightingale, photographed in 1856, when she was 36 years old.

In 1818, William and Frances Nightingale married and went to Italy on their honeymoon. They stayed in Italy for three years and both their daughters were born there. Their first daughter, Parthenope, was named after the old name for the city of Naples, where she was born. On the 12th of May 1820, their second daughter was born. She was also named after the Italian city of her birth. Her parents named her Florence.

◀ William and Frances Nightingale, Florence's parents.

▶A painting of the city of Florence, at about the time Florence Nightingale was born there.

The Nightingales and their baby daughters returned to England in 1821. They went to live at Lea Hurst, a house near Matlock, in Derbyshire.

When Florence was five years old, her father bought Embley Park, a big house near Romsey, in Hampshire. The family divided their time between their two homes. In the winter they lived at Embley Park. In the summer they lived at Lea Hurst.

Lea Hurst, where Florence lived in the summer. This picture was painted by her sister Parthenope.

Florence and Parthenope were educated at home, like other children from wealthy families. They had a governess to teach them music and drawing. Their father taught them history, mathematics, and how to read and write in different languages.

Florence was clever and she found her school lessons easy. Parthenope preferred painting and needlework.

Florence, aged about 16. She is stitching a piece of embroidery. Parthenope, aged about 17, is standing next to her.

When Florence was 16 years old, something happened that changed her life for ever. It was the 7th of February 1837, and she was in the garden at Embley Park. Suddenly, she thought she heard the voice of God calling to her.

From then on, Florence was certain that God had chosen her for a special purpose. She believed that God wanted her to do His work on Earth – but she did not know what that work could possibly be.

Embley Park and gardens, where Florence heard God's voice.

When Florence was in her early 20s, she started visiting sick people in villages close to her home. She was becoming interested in how they were cared for.

Florence felt sure that God wanted her to work as a nurse. She knew this would be hard for her to do. In the 1840s, nurses came from poor families, not wealthy ones like Florence's.

Many nurses were old and untidy. Most lived in the hospitals where they worked.

When Florence told her parents that she wanted to become a nurse, they were very upset. They decided she should go on holiday with friends, Charles and Selina Bracebridge, in the hope that she would forget about her plans.

Nothing could have been further from the truth. In July 1850, Florence and her friends visited Kaiserswerth, a town in Prussia (now Germany), where there was a famous hospital that trained nurses. The next year, Florence returned to Kaiserswerth and trained as a nurse for three months.

Florence trained to be a nurse here, at the Institution of Deaconesses, in Kaiserswerth, Prussia.

Florence returned to England as a trained nurse. In 1853, she was put in charge of a small hospital in Harley Street, London. At last, Mr and Mrs Nightingale saw that Florence was determined to work as a nurse and decided to help her. As she was not going to be paid to do her new job, her father promised to give her £500 a year, which was a lot of money for the time.

Florence wrote this letter to say she would accept the job at the Harley Street hospital.

Florence worked at the Harley Street hospital for over a year. It was her first real chance to care for the sick. She also showed that she was good at organising things. For example, she had bells placed next to the patients' beds. When patients needed a nurse, they rang their bell. No one had thought of doing this before.

The biggest problem at the hospital was a lack of trained nurses – but something soon happened to change this.

A photograph of Florence taken about the time she worked at the Harley Street hospital.

13

In March 1854, Britain, France and Turkey went to war against Russia in the Crimean War. It was the first war seen by photographers and reporters, and people in Britain were able to read about it in their daily newspapers. This is what William Russell wrote in *The Times*:

> "It is with feelings of surprise and anger that the public will learn that no sufficient preparations have been made for the care of the wounded. Not only are there not sufficient surgeons ... no dressers and nurses ... there is not even linen to make bandages."

William Russell's famous words appeared in *The Times* newspaper on the 12th of October 1854.

Many battles were fought in the Crimean War, and lots of soldiers died or were injured.

People were shocked when they read the news. Something had to be done to care for the sick and wounded British soldiers.

In October 1854, three days after William Russell's report had been printed in *The Times*, Sidney Herbert, the government official in charge of the army, wrote to Florence. He asked her to go to Turkey and take charge of the army's hospitals there.

Florence accepted her new job. Two weeks later, on the 4th of November 1854, she and 38 other nurses reached Scutari, a district in the Turkish city of Constantinople. This was where the British army had its main hospital. At first, the doctors at the hospital did not like the idea of working with women. However, the unexpected arrival of hundreds of injured soldiers from the Battle of Balaclava made them ask Florence and her nurses for their help.

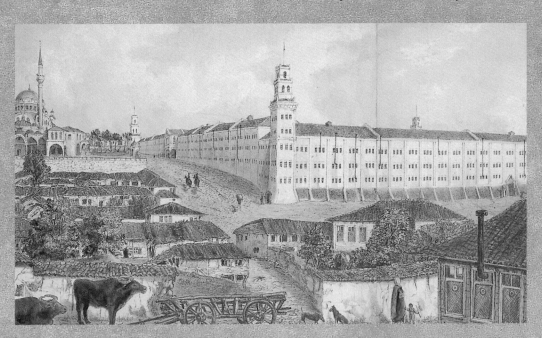

The Barrack Hospital in Scutari was the British army's main hospital.

Florence soon set up a timetable for her nurses to follow. She took charge of the hospital stores and filled them with bandages and medicines. She had the hospital drains cleaned and mended, and improved the water supply. The patients were given clean sheets to lie on, and good food to eat. Florence became the soldiers' friend, and they called her "the lady with a lamp", after the lantern she carried at night.

▲ It was a lantern like this one that Florence carried.

◀ Florence and wounded soldiers in the Barrack Hospital.

The Crimean War ended in 1856, and Florence returned to England a heroine. The government asked her for advice on improving the health of the army. She wrote a report that said soldiers died because army hospitals were dirty, unhygienic places where diseases spread. Her report made the army clean up its hospitals. Florence also worked hard at finding ways of improving the health of people in India. She described her thoughts and ideas in a famous book called *Notes on Nursing*.

People bought souvenirs like this of Florence to put in their homes.

Florence's most important work was in turning nursing into a career that women would be proud to do. First, though, they had to be trained to work as nurses.

In 1860, Florence set up the Nightingale Training School for nurses. It was based at St Thomas's Hospital, London, and its nurses became known as Nightingale Nurses. After being trained for a year, they began their work in hospitals. The Nightingale Nurses spread Florence's ideas about nursing around the world.

Mrs Sarah Wardroper was chosen by Florence to train the first Nightingale Nurses.

In thanks for her life of hard work, Florence received many awards. Queen Victoria gave her the Royal Red Cross. King Edward the Seventh gave her the Order of Merit. It was the first time it had ever been given to a woman.

Florence Nightingale died on the 13th of August 1910. More than 1,000 nurses, and many old soldiers from the Crimean War went to her funeral at St. Paul's Cathedral, London.

Florence, aged 66, with a group of her Nightingale Nurses.

Important dates

1820 Florence Nightingale was born in Florence, Italy.

1837 Age 16 – she believed she heard the voice of God.

1846 Age 26 – she began teaching herself about hospitals.

1851 Age 31 – she trained to be a nurse at Kaiserswerth, Prussia.

1853 Age 33 – she became Superintendent of the Institution for the Care of Sick Gentlewomen in Distressed Circumstances, in Harley Street, London.

1854 Age 34 – Crimean War began. She was put in charge of the army's hospitals in Turkey.

1856 Age 36 – Crimean War ended.

1859 Age 39 – she wrote a book called *Notes on Nursing*.

1860 Age 40 – the Nightingale Training School for nurses opened at St. Thomas's Hospital, London.

1910 Age 90 – Florence Nightingale died.

Keywords

dresser
an old word for a person who put bandages on people

governess
a woman who teaches children at home

heroine
a woman who does brave and important things and is admired by many people

Order of Merit
an award given to people who have done great work for their country

surgeon
a doctor who performs operations on sick or injured people

unhygienic
something that is dirty and carries germs

Index